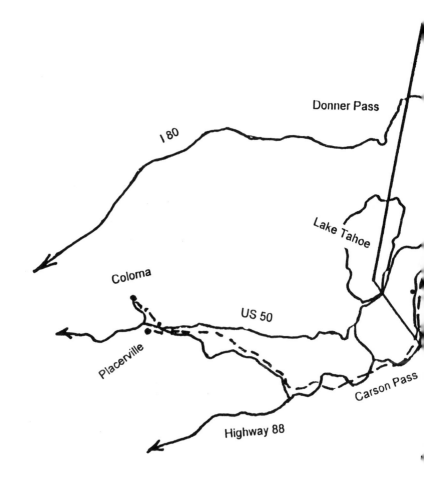

Donner Pass

I 80

Lake Tahoe

Coloma

US 50

Placerville

Carson Pass

Highway 88

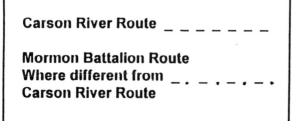

Carson River Route _ _ _ _ _ _ _

Mormon Battalion Route
Where different from _ . _ . _ . _ .
Carson River Route

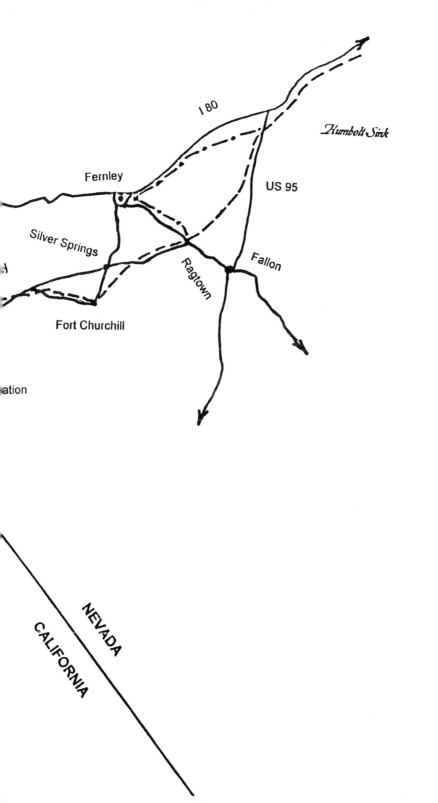

GOLD RUSH TRAIL

A Guide to the Carson River Route

of the Emigrant Trail

Woodfords CA
by way of Highway 88
to
Mormon Emigrant Trail Road
(Referred to as Iron Mountain Road before 1990)

To Shanon & Gus,
Enjoy the Trail.
My best
Frank Tortorich
9-28-99

Published by
Wagon Wheel Tours
1998

I dedicate this my first writing experience
to my loving wife
Mary Ann
My special rose

Published by Wagon Wheels tours
12544 Eldel Road, Pine Grove CA 95665-9718
(209) 296-7242

ISBN 0-9662907-0-4

This book was written to commemorate the Sesquicentennial
of the opening of the Carson River Route

Printed and assisted by Barry Duncan of Mother Lode Printing

CONTENTS

ACKNOWLEDGMENTS

The GOLD RUSH TRAIL guide book was written with support and encouragement given by many people.

My major champion was my best friend and wife, Mary Ann, who joined me on every phase of the book. She did the word processing and cut & paste work so it magically came to some kind of order. On many trips she repeatedly checked odometer readings and directions. She has been my partner during our 20 some years researching the Trail.

Phyllis Hewett is next in line for my appreciation. Her talent and skill in proof-reading to correct my feeble attempt at the English language deserves my most sincere thanks.

Carol Tortorich for proofing the final, final, final, honest final copy.

A special recognition goes to David Bigler who read the manuscript for historical accuracy and offered some sage advice that immensely helped me develop my writing style. Dave is a descendant of Ezariah Smith, one of the party of Mormons who opened the Carson River Route for wagon travel. He is the editor of Ezariah's journal, *THE GOLD RUSH JOURNAL OF EZARIAH SMITH.*

And to Glenn Gottshalls, Amador District Ranger of the Eldorado National Forest, neighbor and friend, who in 1978 encouraged me to sign that first Volunteer Agreement to do Emigrant Trail research for his office. It was the beginning of a wondrous journey for me.

It was John and Patty Brissenden of Sorensen's Resort in Hope Valley who gave me the incredible opportunity to give programs and lead tours along the very same trail that the Mormons opened in 1848 and the pioneers followed.

To my son Michael who spent many summers hiking and locating the Trail with me. He showed great kindness to this old man by being such a great sport in driving practice runs to check the guide's accuracy and to see if the directions were clear enough.

OCTA has gifted me with numerous friends who have generously shared their trail knowledge and book publishing skills. To those folks go my deepest gratitude.

And I would be remiss if I didn't recognize the support of the many other people, some strangers, who encouraged me to write this trail guide.   Frank Tortorich, Jr.

PREFACE

As early as the 1820s United States citizens have been coming overland to Alta California. The only routes into California at that time were south from Oregon or north from southern California by way of Mexican territory. The Sierra Nevada presented an impassable barrier to all but the Native Americans.

In 1827 Jedediah Smith came into California through southern California on a trapping and exploring expedition. Smith left California crossing over the Sierra somewhere near Ebbetts Pass. He left no blazed trail or usable description of the route.

Joseph Walker came to California in 1833 over the Sierra near Yosemite. He, too, left no usable migration route.

The Bartleson-Bidwell party of 1841 was the first organized wagon train. Since the group abandoned all their wagons in eastern Nevada and barely survived the ordeal, they left no wagon trail nor any trace of their travel through the Sierra.

The first route used by wagons over the great Sierra barrier was in 1844. This route was opened by the Murphy-Stephens-Townsend party. They followed down the Humboldt River in Nevada. Using local Indian guides, they were able to find a wagon route up the Truckee River and over the Sierra through a pass that later was referred to as Donner Pass.

It was 1846 when the Donners were trapped in the snow just below the pass that would soon bear their name.

With the desire to *Go West* came the promise of free farm land in a most agreeable climate. Many prominent people in the government thought that the United States should possess all the land from the Atlantic Ocean to the Pacific Ocean.

By the 1840s *Manifest Destiny* was on the lips of many. The mood of the day was that the land is ours for the taking and no one had the right to stop us. This same attitude viewed the Native Americans as a nuisance to be disposed of if they got in the way.

The wagon train migration began to Oregon in 1843. Only a token few were headed to the Mexican territory of California.

The discovery of gold in 1848 would not only change the destination of the pioneers, it would change the entire mood of a nation.

Before gold was discovered, the Overland route to the West was referred to as the Oregon Trail. Those going to California would take the California cut-off just west of Fort Hall (Pocatello, Idaho). After the discovery of gold, most pioneers were heading for California and people began referring to the trail as the California Trail.

There were three possible choices branching from the Humboldt River in Nevada in 1848.

The first was the Applegate-Lassen Route. This much longer route took the gold seekers too far north.

The second was the Truckee River Route, also known as the Donner Route. This route not only had an unfortunate reputation, it was a very difficult trail over the Sierra Nevada.

The third was known as the Carson River Route. This route was the shortest trail to the gold fields and the most popular trail between 1848 and 1851.

By 1851 other cut-offs were opened. Some of these trails were easier over the mountains and shorter to the gold fields. This same year also experienced the beginning of commercially-built toll roads. The Johnson Cut Off over Echo Summit near Lake Tahoe (US Highway 50) was one such road.

Over the years these routes were referred to by various names. The Carson River Route has been referred to in recent times as the Carson Pass Trail or The Mormon-Carson Trail. One segment of this route is listed on highway markers as the Mormon Emigrant Trail. All of these various names invite confusion.

For simplicity we will use the name the emigrants used, the Carson River Route.

This guide book offers a brief introduction into the history during the westward migration.

It is hoped that those folks who may enjoy following this guide and experiencing the Trail evidence that exists after all these years will become excited and want to learn more.

Two brief lists of books of general interest about the Carson River Route and related historical information are provided in the back of this guide book.

INTRODUCTION

This guide book is designed to lead people along 33 miles of the historic Emigrant Trail which are easily accessible along California State Highway 88 from the town of Woodfords to Mormon Emigrant Trail Road.

Most segments run parallel to Highway 88 and are found a short walk from the pavement. The walking segments range in length from a few yards to just under 2 miles. The longer segments usually can be reached from two end sites. These sections can be walked halfway from each end, thereby reducing the round trip distances.

It is possible to follow the entire 33 miles in one day. To do each segment thoroughly, taking photographs and experiencing the spirit of the Trail, you may need several days. It all depends on individual preferences.

Some people may wish to revisit some segments during the different seasons of the year. Early spring exposes the bare ground where trail evidence is obvious. Summer can hide the Trail as the grass and brush grows lush and full. Fall often offers a splash of vibrant colors and winter will find the Trail buried with snow.

Some segments like Devil's Ladder will be difficult for some, so common sense is necessary. Each person should know his/her limitations. I have seen people in their eighties and early nineties hike this steep section of the Trail. The key is to take your time and not to overextend yourself.

Most of this trail is above 7,000 feet. Carson Pass is 8,576 feet.

It is best not to do hard hiking at these elevations the first day you are in the mountains. Give yourself one day for your internal body pressures to adjust to the higher elevations.

The one segment of the Trail that is not near Highway 88 is the segment over West Pass along Squaw Ridge. Because this segment does not meet the criterion of being easily accessible from Highway 88, it has been omitted from this guidebook.

Information on this segment is available from the United States Forest Service (USFS) visitors' station at Carson Pass, USFS field offices, knowledgeable people, or hiking guides of the area.

Or in this author's next guide book?

TERMS AND DEFINITIONS

Depression: A low spot in the ground, like a swale but not as deep.

Emigrant: One who leaves their native country, i.e. leaving the United States. Versus the immigrant who is one that enters a country not their native land.

Elevation: Numbers are given in feet above sea level.

Groove: There are numerous locations where wagon wheels have actually worn a notch into rocks and boulders, leaving cuts.

Highway/highway: The upper case "H" in Highway is used to denote present day State Highway 88. While the lower case "h" in highway is used to denote the old Highway 88.

Pioneer: One who ventures into unknown or unclaimed territory to settle.

Polish: Thousands of slow-moving wagon wheels rubbed against the same rock, leaving the rock smooth or polished.

Pristine: This is the best of all trail evidence. A pristine segment of the Trail has had no impacts since wagons stopped using it. See Trail Classifications.

Road: A route where earth was moved to level to the ground. This is a constructed, maintained and significantly improved travel way, e.g., Amador-Carson Valley Wagon Road.

Rust stain or iron oxide stain: This feature is most often found with the polished rock. As the wagon wheel rubbed and smoothed the rock, iron from the wagon wheels left a tiny iron deposit on the rock. This tiny deposit would oxidize or rust, leaving a stain of rust on the rock. Not all polished rocks have rust stains.

Seeing the Elephant: The term *Seeing the Elephant* meant different things to different folks. Most used the term to refer to a great undertaking, such as going to California. Others referred to the Sierra Nevada as *The Elephant* and those folks having crossed the mountains perhaps claimed to have *Conquered the Elephant.*

Sierra Nevada: A mountain range bordering 400 miles of the northern part of the eastern side of the state of California. Sierra means a rugged range of mountains. Nevada means snow covered. Incorrectly the use of the name of Sierra Nevada mountains is like saying Snow covered mountain range mountains.

Swale: A "U" shaped depression in the ground left by wagons, animals and people eroding away the soil. Weather usually adds to the erosion.

Trace: This term is used to indicate that very little Trail evidence can be found. With close searching subtle evidence may be seen.

Trail: This term with upper case "T" will be used to refer to the Carson River Route of the Emigrant Trail.

Trail: A route where people, wagons and animals could travel. Slight improvements were made, such as moving rocks or logs, cutting small trees and brush. Doing a minimal amount of work, e.g., Emigrant Trail.

Trail Classification: Trails are rated from Class I to Class V. A Class I trail has the best evidence, is usually easy to see and locate and is the same as Pristine. Whereas a Class V trail means no evidence is left at all and only the approximate route is known. All other classifications are degrees from Class I to Class V.

Two-track: Eroded areas left in the soil are usually created by modern day vehicles.

Silver Lake Campers Association

Large Can Lid

Square Aluminum

Small Can Lid

EMIGRANT ROAD   SLCA   Strip Sign

CARSON EMIGRANT TRAIL

Pregnant Triangle

Diamond Trail

U.S. Forest Service

TRAIL MARKERS AND SIGNS

Over the years, various groups have placed markers along the Emigrant Trail to assist modern day explorers in finding the trail.

Markers: In the 1940s and 1950s a group called the Silver Lake Campers Association (SLCA) placed a series of markers along this segment of Trail. Used in conjunction with the strip signs, the SLCA used aluminum coffee can lids, 3 inch aluminum squares, and 2 1/2 inch can lids painted orange. These were nailed on trees in a line of sight direction.
Many above listed signs and markers are no longer in place due to vandals and snow.

Strip Signs: The SLCA's main sign was a white metal rectangular sign 4 inches high and 18 inches long. Painted on this sign were the words EMIGRANT ROAD and letters SLCA in black. These strip signs were nailed on trees parallel to the Trail.

United States Forest Service Signs: In the 1970s the USFS placed 6 inch by 15 inch metal signs along the Trail. These signs were painted yellow with brown letters reading CARSON EMIGRANT TRAIL. It also pictured a pine tree and an ox drawn wagon. Some of these are still in place.

Pregnant Triangle Markers: The USFS has also installed the 3 1/2 inch white "pregnant" triangles indicating the Trail as a USA National Recreation Trail. Some of these are still in place.
In 1998 the United States Park Service plans to install 4 inch pregnant triangles with the words CALIFORNIA TRAIL National Historic Trail, with an ox yoke printed upon it.

Diamond Markers: USFS has also installed the standard 4 inch by 5 inch white diamond trail markers. This is the most reliable of all the markers.

Brown Iron "T" Markers: These are not in the photo on page x. Each of these brown painted iron markers are made from railroad track and have an inscribed plaque bolted to them. They stand about 3 feet above the ground and the cross member is about 18 inches wide.

In the 1970s the Nevada State Historical Markers Association began to place a series of markers along the Carson River Route from the Humboldt Sink to West Pass about every 5 miles. In more recent years a group named Trails West picked up where the Nevada marking group ended.

There will be five of these markers along this section of Trail. Beginning at Snowshoe Spring and ending at Mormon Emigrant Trail Road turn off.

Altogether there are about nine different types of signs or markers along the Trail. The USFS plans to reduce the number of markers to three or four different markers. The SLCA strip sign, the white trail diamond, the pregnant triangles and possibly the aluminum squares are to be the official signs.

PUBLIC LAND

All Trail segments listed in this guide will be on Public Land. This guide will indicate where the private segments are located. **Never will this guide direct anyone to trespass on private property.** The Pacific Gas and Electric Company owns some land which the Trail crosses, but since it is a public utility, their land is open to public travel.

If someone is in doubt about the boundaries of public or private land, the best choice is not to cross the segment in question.

... We took the Carson Route, as it was considered the safest. Had the Donner party kept to the old emigrant trail they would have escaped the terrible tragedy which befell them ...
Mary E. Ackley, 1852

GOLD RUSH TRAIL

A Brief History
Of the Opening of
The Carson River Route

The Carson River Route was not opened nor discovered by Kit Carson as the name would indicate. Kit Carson was in this area in January 1844 with the exploring party of John C. Fremont. Carson was officially hired by Fremont as a hunter and Indian fighter but not as his guide as many think. Thomas "Broken Hand" Fitzpatrick was hired as the guide. In earlier years he had been exploring in the Great Basin and had a basic but limited knowledge of the area.

Carson did come to California in 1829 with Ewing Young on a trapping expedition traveled as far north as Mount Diablo but never in the Sierra Nevada. Carson had entered California through the southern route into California and left by the same trail.

However, on his 1844 expedition, Fremont did name the Carson River for his friend Kit. Fremont had great respect for his friend and wanted to honor him in this way.

Because of the deep snow in January and February of 1844 no trace of a route was left as they crossed the mountains somewhere near Carson Pass. They did not realize this would ever be considered as a viable wagon route.

Then, how did this become the Gold Rush Trail?

To answer this question we must go back to the year 1846 and examine the events occurring in the country.

First, the United States declared war on Mexico on May 13. This included Alta California as well as the Republic of Texas..

Secondly, the Donner-Reed wagon train party was preparing to depart for California.

Thirdly, the Mormons were being driven out of their home at Nauvoo, Illinois, where their persecutions were escalating. In order to save their lives and to continue their religious practices, Brigham Young, the leader of the Mormon Church, felt their only choice was

1

to leave Nauvoo. He planned to establish a new settlement some place west of the Rocky Mountains in the wilderness.

Young lead the Saints across the frozen Mississippi River on February 9, 1846.

On that same day, a young Elder in the Church, Sam Brannan, sailed out of New York Harbor on the ship *Brooklyn*. On board were 235 men, women and children, mostly Mormons, plus equipment and supplies necessary to establish a new settlement. Brannan's destination was Yerba Buena, the name for San Francisco then. It was Brannan's dream to establish the new Zion in California.

As the main group of Mormons struggled across Iowa, the war with Mexico was heating up. President Polk sent troops to Texas and sent naval ships to the Pacific along the coast of Alta California.

Just before arriving at the Missouri River, Brigham Young would receive a request from President Polk to form a battalion of five hundred men to fight the war in the West, meaning California.

Young was agreeable to this request. However, not everyone in the Church would agree. Many would argue that the Mormons should not help a country that did little to protect the Mormon people from persecution. Some Church members believed it was a US Government plot to set up the Mormon men to be killed in the War and thus decrease the population of the Mormons.

Likewise, some in Congress did not agree that the Government should seek help from this "despicable" group of people. Polk argued that there was a need for troops and here was a willing group. Young, on the other hand, had to sell his people on this idea. Young's argument was no matter where they went they would be under the control of the United States Government and to remember this was their country, too. He went on to tell the elders this was an opportunity for them to show the country they were good citizens, hard working, dependable, honest, dedicated people. Young also reminded the elders of their need for money.

The Army not only would pay each battalion member but they could later keep their Army issue.

Young was able to convince the Elders and the Church people to form a Mormon Battalion. Five hundred men would enlist. Twenty women would also enlist as washer women.

Many of the enlisted men were married and were naturally concerned for the care their wives and children. Wherefore, approximately ninety non-battalion women and children would go along. Other men left their wives and children in the care of family members or friends. The Battalion was mustered into the Army at Fort Leavenworth, Kansas, the first part of August 1846. They began preparing for their six-month march to San Diego. The Battalion would be under the command of General Stephen Watts Kearny and his Army of the West.

Young gave directions to the Battalion members on how to create their own military structure. They formed five companies of one hundred, this would be subdivided into companies of fifty, and these subdivided into companies of ten. Each company had a captain. This is the same organization that Young used during the Mormon mass migrations west.

The first companies began their march along the Santa Fe Trail on August 13 with the rest soon to follow.

The ship *Brooklyn*, with Sam Brannan's party, sailed into San Francisco Bay on July 31, 1846, three weeks after the United States Naval Fleet took Monterey and Yerba Buena.

After some discussion between Brannan and American Naval officers, the Mormons from the *Brooklyn* were allowed to land. Brannan, like Young, took little time in organizing his people.

He dispatched one group up the San Joaquin River to begin farming in a place they named New Hope. This is about 1 mile up the Stanislaus River from the San Joaquin River.

Most of the party settled in Yerba Buena.

Later, others would settle in the San Jose valley to farm.

By now, Young knew it was too late in the year to continue the migration west. Plans were made to build a town. This temporary settlement called Winter Quarters was just north of the present city of Omaha. Streets were named, log cabins built, fields plowed and corrals constructed. Here the Saints would spend a miserable winter with several hundred members dying. They began to make plans for the travel to the Great Salt Lake the following year.

By mid-August the Donner-Reed party would begin to realize that time was getting late and they might have trouble getting to

California before the snow blocked the Sierra. And yet, they still had the Wasatch Mountains and the Salt Desert to cross, with California still some 700 arduous miles away.

By December 1846 the news of the Donner-Reed party trapped in the Sierra snow reached the towns of California. Plans were being made for their rescue. However, it would not be until that April before the last of the survivors of the Donner party would be rescued from their ordeal in the mountains.

On January 29, 1847, only four women and 338 members of the Mormon Battalion straggled into San Diego. Others that had become sick or injured were sent to Fort Pueblo, a trading post in present day Colorado, to spend the winter and to recover. Some would die along this most grueling of marches.

The last battle of the Mexican War fought in California was on January 8, 1847 nearly a month before the Battalion arrived. Nevertheless, they would stay on as an occupation force in southern California for six months.

Sam Brannan would travel east in April of 1847 to meet with Brigham Young. Brannon planned to convince Young to bring the Saints to California.

Brannan met Young on the Green River, in Wyoming, and began to present his case for California. But Young would not waver from his plan to settle in the Salt Lake Valley. He would tell Brannan that there were too many people in California, and only in the wilderness could they practice their religion in peace.

Young also told Brannan to return to California to tell the Battalion members after their discharge they were to remain and work in California until the following year. Young knew that times were going to be hard and food would be scarce in the Salt Lake Valley that first year.

On July 16, 1847, one year after their enlistment, the Battalion was discharged. Some reenlisted and remained in southern California.

A group of 51 headed up the coast of California to meet with the people of the Brannan settlement in Yerba Buena, which was just beginning to be called San Francisco.

A few returned east by the route they came to reunite with families.

The largest group, consisting of 223 members, headed north through the central California. Their destination was Sutter's Fort for supplies before traveling east over the Sierra via the Truckee River Route (Donner Pass).

Of the four women who reached California with the Battalion, one would die in California, two were wives of men who reenlisted for another year. The fourth one, the washer woman Melissa Coray with her husband, became members of the fifty-one traveling up the coast of California to Yerba Buena.

A large group of 223 Mormons left Sutter's Fort on August 29 well supplied and began their travel east with high hopes for now they were going home.

After four or five days, the group camped on the west side of the Sierra crest near Soda Springs. There they met Sam Brannan returning from the Salt Lake Valley. He described to the discharged soldiers the place Young had decided to settle.

Continuing east over the mountains, they came upon the grizzly remains of the Donner-Reed camp. There the group met Captain Brown with the official written orders from Brigham Young.

The orders read that the Battalion members should stay in California another year and only those men who had family responsibilities should continue. About one hundred would continue east while the others returned to California to seek work.

Sutter hired about eighty of the discharged Battalion men. Some were sent to build a grist mill about 15 miles east of the fort.

Six were sent, with James Marshall, 45 miles east up the American River to build a saw mill in a beautiful valley called Coloma. It was here in Coloma where James Marshall discovered gold in the tailrace of the mill.

Marshall always thought he had discovered gold on January 19, 1848. However, the journals of the Mormons would set the discovery date at January 24, 1848. Many of these men kept accurate journals from the day they left Fort Leavenworth until they reached the Salt Lake Valley. Some men even continued to keep journals after reaching the Salt Lake Valley.

Word of the discovery of gold spread to the discharged Battalion men working at the grist mill at Natomas. They prospected successfully and found gold at a place soon to be called Mormon Island, now under water in Folsom Lake.

The Mormons at Coloma continued to build the saw mill and only prospected for gold in their spare time. Some did quite well but gold would not keep them in California.

By the spring of 1848 some of the discharged Battalion Mormon members began making plans to travel to the Salt Lake Valley.

A camp was set up on June 18, 1848, to assemble all supplies and equipment needed not only for the trip to the Salt Lake Valley but for use at the new settlement. This camp was in a pleasant valley just east of present day Placerville. The name Pleasant Valley still stands today.

A few miles east of Pleasant Valley, James Sly built a corral in a beautiful place he claimed looked like a park. This name Sly Park is also used today.

On July 3, 1848, forty-five men and one woman with seventeen wagons, one hundred fifty oxen, one hundred fifty horses and mules hauling supplies, equipment and two brass cannons, began the great journey east.

The group did not want to use the Truckee River Route for they knew how difficult that route was furthermore it carried the pall of the Donner-Reed tragedy. Consequently, they headed up the Sierra ridges looking for a different route. By following Indian trails, this advance group found a new way over the mountains.

A scouting party of three men went ahead to explore the trail but never returned to rejoin the main group.

The going was difficult as trees had to be cut, brush cleared and boulders rolled out of the way. Despite these difficulties the group moved along 6 to 10 miles a day. Some layover days were necessary when work on the trail became more difficult.

On July 16 the Mormons camped by a creek. And on July 17 at a spring where wild onions or leeks were growing. The names given both these places by this group were Camp Creek and Leek Springs and are both still in use today.

From the camp at Leek Springs, they worked the trail for several miles when they came to another spring. Here they found the ground disturbed. James Sly said it looked like a grave and speculated that their three missing scouts might be buried there.

On July 19 they broke camp at Leek Springs, and moved up the mountain to the other spring. With tools from their wagon, they

6

carefully dug into the disturbed ground and discovered their three friends in the shallow grave. Their bodies were stripped of all clothing and riddled with arrows. Saddened with what they found, a new grave was dug and the bodies reburied. An inscription was carved on a tree, "To the memory of Daniel Browett, Ezrah H. Allen, Henderson Cox, who was supposed to have been murdered and buried by Indians on the night of 27 June 1848." The mourners named the place Tragedy Spring. It still holds that sad name.

The next eight days would take the group to the highest point wagons would ever travel during the westward migration, West Pass. This backbone of the Sierra Nevada is 9,600 feet.

On July 30 the Mormon group crossed the second summit of 8,576 feet. This summit is now referred to as Carson Pass.

As they were descending on the east side of the Sierra they came to a beautiful valley. Here they felt real hope they could, in fact, complete their journey. They named the place Hope Valley, another name that is still used today.

At the lower end of Hope Valley, the group had to camp for seven days while men cut trees and moved logs and boulders to make way for their wagons through river canyon. This would be the most difficult segment of the Carson River Route.

Finally on August 4, 1848, emerging from the canyon, they followed the Carson River ultimately striking out over the desert. Then, not certain of the route, the group turned north-west near Ragtown to find the Truckee River. They reached it near present day Wadsworth, Nevada, and then proceeded east to the Humboldt Sink.

Near some boiling springs on August 15, the group met a mountain man named James Clyman heading for California. Clyman was leading a train of eighteen wagons intending to use the Truckee Route. The Mormons showed him the gold they found and gave him a map showing their new, easier route to California which he used.

The next day the group met Pierre Cornwall leading twenty-five wagons. The same story was told to Cornwall and he also used the new trail.

They met Peter Lassen on August 26. However he was heading north to use the Applegate Route that was opened in 1846 as an alternate route to Oregon.

On August 30, they met Joseph Chiles with forty-eight wagons.

Chiles not only took their advice but improved on the route. Knowing the area, he took a short cut from the Humboldt Sink directly to the Carson River. Chiles had been through this area in 1841 when he first came to California with the Bartleson-Bidwell party.

On October 6, 1848, this motley group of Mormons would finally reach the Salt Lake Valley.

Other Mormon parties followed using this route later that same year.

No one yet knows exactly how many others used the Carson River Route that first year. From journals we can speculate that more than one hundred-twenty wagons with approximately five to seven hundred people and perhaps fifteen hundred to two thousand animals traveled this route in 1848.

The Carson River Route gained instant popularity. Although it was higher in elevation than the Truckee River Route, the travel was incredibly easier on men and animals. The Carson River canyon (Woodfords) required only three river crossings compared to the Truckee River canyon which could require twenty-seven river crossings or more.

The gold rush began in 1849 with over twenty thousand people coming to California using the Carson River Route.

A peak year was 1850, with fifty thousand people coming west, most using the Carson River Route.

In the years to follow, other routes would open to other gold "diggins" and traffic would slow on the Carson River Route.

However, in 1859 a second rush would occur when silver was discovered in Virginia City, Nevada. Many in California, seeking their fortune, would travel east by way of the Carson River Route.

In a very short time, realignments and improvements would be made to the Carson River Route and by 1860 it would be known as the Amador-Carson Valley Wagon Road.

Eventually, this route, which began five thousand to ten thousand years ago as an Indian trading and travel route, would become California State Highway Route 88.

A Guide to the Carson River Route

of the Emigrant Trail

Woodfords CA
to
Mormon Emigrant Trail Road
(Referred to as Iron Mountain Road before 1990)

Distances listed refer to your vehicle odometer readings from the last point to the next point along the Highway only. They will not include any side trips mentioned in the guide. Reset the odometer as you enter the Highway as directed. In some cases the mileages will be continuous and this will be clearly noted when appropriate.

Distances are approximate due to slight differences in odometers.

By giving reset odometer readings, you should be able to find the Trail at any location without having to start at the beginning of the guide.

Descriptions, maps and photographs are included to make it easier for you to discover the different locations.

Directions will be indicated as east or west because this is the overall direction of travel. Directions along Highway 88 will be given as east or west even though this may not always be the compass direction. For example, Highway 88 in Hope Valley actually travels in north and south compass directions. On US maps even numbered highways generally travel in east and west directions, while all odd numbered highways generally travel in a north and south directions.

The letters in bold - **(S)** - before some odometer readings - **1.2** - denote places where the suggested walking segments are located. and correspond with letters on appropriate section maps.

A scattering of diary entries are included to enhance your ability to experience the spirit of the Trail.

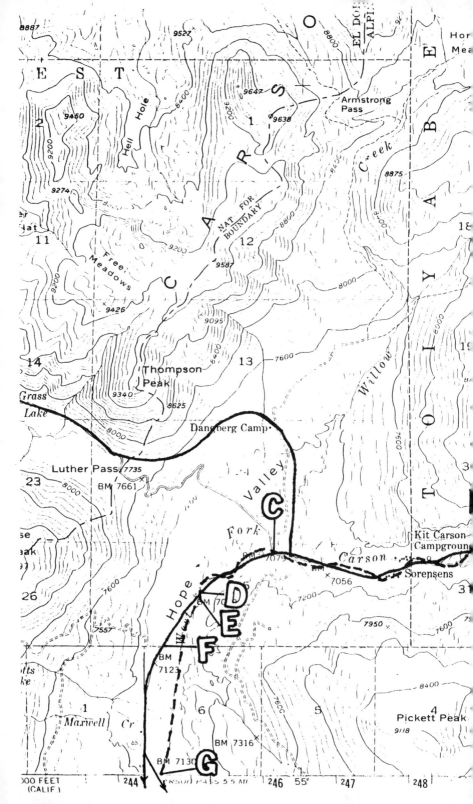

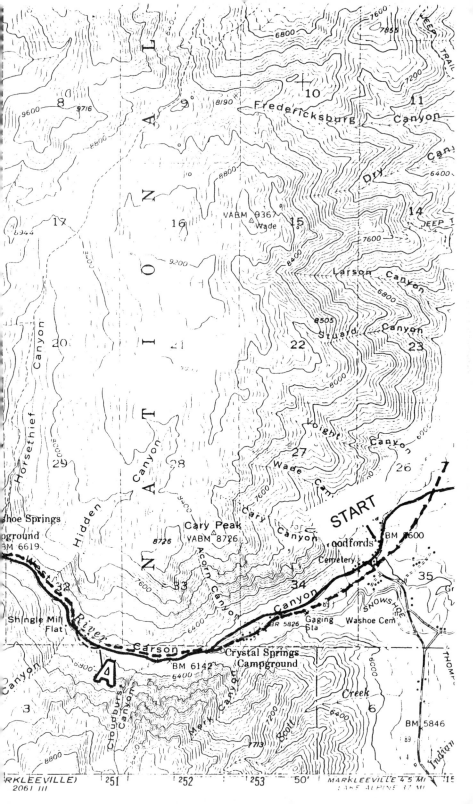

Carson Canyon and Hope Valley Section

Start   Pony Express Marker

This marker is on the bypass road just west of the store and restaurant at Woodfords Station. This is part of the old highway.

Beginning the tour here you can experience the evolution of this historic route. The Trail has seen many changes over the last 150 years. In 1848 it began as a wagon trail taking Mormons to Salt Lake Valley and bringing emigrants and gold seekers to California. In 1859 when silver was discovered in Nevada, the Trail became a commercially constructed road known as the Amador-Carson Valley Wagon Road. In 1860 it was used as a transcontinental mail route for five weeks, better known as the Pony Express Route. Over the years improvements were made leading to the modern highway we now enjoy. But let us not forget that this was first an Indian trade and travel route that some say date back five to ten thousand years.

<u>Proceed west on this old highway segment for a short distance until its end, where it rejoins the Highway. Reset your odometer to zero, proceed west and drive to the Crystal Springs Road.</u>

.8 Crystal Springs Road <u>Turn left and cross the Carson River.</u> The bridge over the Carson River is at the same location as First Crossing. This is the first of three crossings the emigrants made in the Carson Canyon. You are now on the old highway and the Trail.

<u>Continue west to the stop sign that rejoins the Highway. Reset the odometer and proceed west.</u>

Look for some old pavement to your right and below the Highway. This is the old highway and approximates the Emigrant Trail. Faint traces can be found in a few locations in these areas.

(A)   1.2   <u>Turn left just west of where the passing lane ends. Take this driveway-like exit and park.</u>

This is a short walking segment of about 250 yards one-way. Follow the wagon road to your left, moving slightly uphill and parallel to the Highway. The Trail stayed above the river because the canyon became narrow and steep in this section. Follow the Trail until it arrives at its end just above the Highway.

*..... After about 30 miles up the river we came to the Carson
Canyon, one of the worst pieces of road on the whole route;
it took us all day with men and animals ever did to make five
miles. No one thought of riding. I carried my baby and
walked all the way.....*
Reminiscences of Mary Jane Walker Caples journey of 1849

<u>Backtrack to your vehicle, return to the Highway, reset the odometer
and proceed west.</u>
To the right there are more segments of the old highway.

.2   Old highway bridge - Second Crossing <u>Turn right and
cross the old highway bridge.</u> This is the approximate location of
Second Crossing the wagons had to make in the canyon. The old
pavement is the approximate location of the Trail. With very few
visible segments from here to Snowshoe Springs campground, <u>return
to the Highway; reset the odometer and proceed west.</u>

(B)   .9   Horsethief Canyon trail head <u>Turn right into the
trail head parking area just past the entrance to Snowshoe Springs
campground that is on the left.</u>
14

<u>Pull off to your right onto a large sandy area and park.</u> This walking segment is about one fourth mile one-way. This will take about 45 minutes round trip depending on your rate of travel.

Start at the brown iron "T" marker with an information plaque. This next segment will be somewhat strenuous, so take your time. Don't forget to take water, camera, insect repellent and other personal items.

While facing the metal "T" marker, proceed to your left on what appears to be an old roadbed for about 80 yards and cross a small stream (usually 18 inches wide) to your left. Walk between the large trees and veer right.

...October 12, 1850 The scenery of this can[y]on exceeds all I have yet seen. There is only room for the road and the river running close by its side...

Franklin Langworthy

15

Stay to the right of a large boulder about 40 yards past the stream and enter a small open grassy area. Do not follow the old service road bed that goes to the left as it will dead end.

After entering the grassy area, walk to your right uphill for 25 yards.

Veering left you will find an opening in the willows. As you pass through a wet area, use the stepping stones if you can find them in the grass.

Continue through an aspen grove to a large metal lid in the ground. This is part of the water system for the campground, and a good place to catch your breath.

Resume you walk uphill passing by a power pole and as you come to an open area, look to your right about 30 yards.

Upon the tall split-face rock is an inscription. It reads:

"ROGERS AUG. 28 49."

This name was written in axle grease. It is very faint and if the sun is shining on it, the letters are extremely difficult to see but it becomes visible if you shade the letters.

Just as you enter the open area you may notice a metal fence post with a small sign indicating that this is a University of Nevada water test area.

Continue up the hill from the fence post walking slightly to your right for 15 yards. You should now see some boulders with some rust stains and polish left by the wagon wheels. You are now standing in the wagon Trail.

Walk for another 45 yards and the Trail will make a gentle "S" turn in this area, first left and then right.

... Graves are numerous on this side of the desert. The usual mode of burying the dead is to dig a very shallow grave, inter the corpse without a coffin, and set up a narrow piece of board by way of a monument on which a brief inscription is cut with a knife ...

Franklin Langworthy, October 5th, 1850

18

Rust-stained Rock

Still facing up hill to your right is a boulder about 2 feet high and 6 feet long with a vertical flat face running parallel to the Trail. This rock has some good samples of the polish and stains made by the wagon wheels. Rub these areas and notice the smooth area. Now rub the back side of the rock and notice its roughness. There are numerous samples of this type of Trail evidence all along this segment.

While looking at this rock, turn around 180 degrees and see "Snowshoe Thompson's Cave."

... In the afternoon, entering a valley between high mountains, we followed it for a time until we reached a narrow gap or can[y]on, where we began the ascent of the Sierras. A turbulent mountain stream spanned by a corduroy bridge was crossed. This, we learned from Mr. Sly, had been built by the Mormon Battalion on its return to Salt Lake ....

Wm. G. Johnston, Friday, July 20th, 1849

Snowshoe Thompson's Cave

This is a large boulder on top of other boulders, leaving a cave like chamber large enough for a person to get out of the weather. It is said that from 1856 to 1876, John "Snowshoe" Thompson carried the mail between Placerville and Genoa twice a month during the winter. Local legend states that Thompson used this shelter when the weather was too severe to travel. The book on the story of Snowshoe is listed in the Suggested Reading section of this guide book.

After exploring the cave, continue up hill, moving a bit to your right. You will see the Trailway between some pine trees.

... At noon we stopped in the can[y]on and took our lunch. Here we met some emigrants, among whom was a lady who lost or left her husband behind. Their horses had been stolen by the Indians, he went after them and never returned ...

Mrs. Margaret Frink, August 24, 1850

From here the Trail curves to the left as you approach the top. When you reach the top look back down to your left and see another very rough wagon Trail coming up among the rocks. If you explore this alternate route you should find more rust stained rocks.

... July 25th. We passed through the can[y]on yesterday and went two miles beyond to camp for the night. The road through this place is rough and rocky beyond conception. Up hill and down hill and over solid blocks of granite as high as the Axel-trees, was the order of the day. ....

William Tell Parker, 1850

Continuing on the Trail, walk over the top of the hill passing under the power lines. As you start down the hill, you will be walking parallel to the power line. After passing under the power lines again, the trail will pass between some very large boulders.

Groove

Polish

The wagons came between these same boulders. You should now be on top of granite rock in the Trail.

Examine these to see the rust stains, grooves and polish. Also, notice the flat, sloping rock to the right and under the bush to see more rust stains, giving visual and physical proof of wagon travel.

From here walk to the Highway by following the footpath that angles a bit to your left over a small rise before descending to the pavement. **Take great care crossing to the other side of the Highway.** From here you will get a view of the old highway and its bridge. This is the location of Third Crossing. From here the Trail climbs through the campground and meets the paved Highway in front of the Hope Valley Resort store.

Some emigrants referred to this canyon as Pass Creek Canyon.

At this point you have two choices. You can follow the Highway back to your vehicle or retrace your steps following the Emigrant Trail back to your vehicle. Backtracking on the Trail is the most interesting as it looks different walking in the return direction.

All distances will be continuous from here. DO NOT RESET THE ODOMETER UNTIL INSTRUCTED TO DO SO.

(OR represents Odometer Reading)

OD   .6   Hope Valley Resort

Hope Valley Resort is just west of the bridge over the Carson River. As you drive west, the Trail will cross to the right side of the Highway. The Trail will recross to the left of the Highway, passing in front of the first cabin at Sorensen's Resort. The Trail passes behind the cafe and past the last cabin. The Trail is marked through Sorensen's Resort.

The Trail will recross the Highway to the right and into Hope Valley. This was the first place the emigrants could camp for the night.

OR   2.0   Burnside Lake Road

Turn left onto the Burnside Lake Road and proceed a short distance passing over the cattle guard. Look for the brown iron "T" marker just to the right of the road in an open area. This is only one of many places the wagons went after they came out of the canyon. The emigrants would fan out over the entire meadow to camp. The wagon groups that followed would have to go farther up the valley in order to find good grass for the animals. By summer's end the entire valley would be grazed off by the thousands of animals that came through.

Return to the Highway, **reset the odometer,** and turn west.

(C)   .2   Picketts Junction on Highway 88

Pull off to the right into the first pullout past the Lake Tahoe turn off (State Route 89). This intersection is known as Picketts Junction. Park and walk through the fence's zig-zag pedestrian gate located just left of the large vehicle gate. You will be walking on segments of old Highway 88 & 89 pavement and the old Picketts Junction.

... Here for the first time on our route the picture of the mountain scenery is fully realized; the mountains close in upon us on every side, and raise their lofty peaks high toward heaven ...

James Abby, Sunday, August 11, 1850

At this old intersection, turn left and walk 30 yards on the old pavement. Now veer to your right and walk parallel to the old pavement. You should now be walking in a Trail swale and see rust marks on some rocks. The Trail runs only 3 or 4 yards parallel to the old pavement. In about 75 yards you will come to small trees growing on the Trail. The soil has been cut by the wagon wheels along the right edge of the Trail. You can follow it until it eventually disappears under the Highway. This piece of Trail is one of the few places where you can see the Emigrant Trail, the old highway, (which was first the Amador-Carson Valley Wagon Road) and present Highway 88 all together.

> *... July 29. Moved across about one mile and half and*
> *camped at what we called Hope Valley, as we now began to*
> *have hope. ...*
>   Henry William Bigler, 1848 (With the first Mormon party.)

Take time to explore this meadow and see what other evidence you can locate. There is a possible emigrant grave in the meadow. Can you find it?

REMEMBER: The taking of any artifacts is violating a Federal Law. So please leave any thing you find for the enjoyment of others.

This is about one third mile one-way if you walk the entire section. If you want to continue to follow the Trail, **CAREFULLY** cross Highway 88 where you last saw the Trail merge with the Highway. Follow it in the same alignment of the Trail when crossing the Highway. On the other side of the Highway, the Trail is easily seen as a berm in a straight line with small trees growing on the Trail. The Trail will enter a grove of pine trees and gently curve back to the Highway in a low area.

Return to your vehicle, reset the odometer and continue west.

(D)   .7   Bridge
Park on the right just before the bridge crossings.
Carefully walk across the Highway and back several yards to see the old roadbed for the Amador-Carson Valley Wagon Road.

This is a nice walking section. Look across the river and to the upstream side of the bridge about 30 yards. You may be able to see the wagon-wide cut into the river bank at the high water mark. This is the spot the wagons crossed the Carson River for the fourth and last time.

(E)   River bank cut <u>To see this better, drive to the west side of the bridge about 50 yards and park on the left of the Highway in front of the broken down gate.</u> Climb through the fence and 3 yards from the fence you will be standing on the Trail.

Riverbank Cut

Walking to the left you will come to the river bank cut that you viewed from the other side. This is a beautiful example of a pristine or Class I Trail.

> *... September 10th, Tuesday (made 10 m.) Cold and cloudy.*
> *After emerging from the Kanyon we strike into a narrow*
> *bottom or valley some 1/4 m wide ... This valley last some 8*
> *miles but little grass, the soil most of the way sandy and*
> *gravelly, timbered with open groves of pine and rather*
> *beautiful ...*
>
> Byron N McKinstry, 1850

As you turn west from the river crossing you will see the Trail continuing west staying just to the left of the fence for about one fourth mile until it disappears into the huge gravel pit used by CAL-TRANS for road construction. Between this fourth river crossing and the gravel pit, the Trail may be difficult to find because of the many vehicles that were driven in this area during the highway construction.

Return to your vehicle, reset the odometer and proceed west.

(F)   .5   Green Gate Drive to the green gate entry way on your left and park. The entire walking segment will be about a mile one-way. Here are some beautiful sections of Trail. This area suffers severe impact from past use as a group campsite, but is still one of best Trail segments in all of Hope Valley.
Climb through the fence and follow the dirt road for 300 yards keeping the gravel pit to your left.

At the end of the 300 yards the dirt road will fork. As you take the right fork you will be on the Trail you will find some strip signs, and some rust and polish on rocks. Along the way keep a sharp eye out for just before you start to break out of the trees, the Trail will veer off to the left parallel the dirt road. It continues through the meadow until it comes to Blue Lakes Road in less than a mile from this point.

Return to your vehicle, reset the odometer and proceed west.

(G) 1.0 Blue Lakes Road
Turn left onto Blue Lakes Road. Drive over the cattle guard and turn left onto a flat gravel area. Drive toward the meadow veering left and drive to the end of the little hill on your left to its end. Park here.

The walk to the far side of the meadow is two thirds mile one-way. The walk is flat and spectacular.

You will see an alignment of about eight small boulders. Walk to the right end of these boulders and you will see the Trail heading eastward across the meadow. You will be at the west end of the segment that started at the green gate.

This section can be very wet in the early part of the spring season due to melting snow. As you walk along this part of the Trail keep a sharp eye for segments of the wagon Trail. It will leave the two-track road, swing off, but stay parallel to, the two-track road. Then it rejoins the two-track road. The two-track road was caused by modern vehicles before the meadow was recently closed to all motorized vehicles. This is a good example of how vehicles followed the same roadway that the wagons used. Enjoy exploring the Meadow.

Return to your vehicle and drive back to Blue Lakes Road.

Turn left on Blue Lakes Road and in .1 of a mile you will see a very old paved roadbed off to your right. Drive straight back into the trees .1 mile and park. The walk is little over one half mile

This is often used as an overflow camping area today. Walk up to the old road bed which is the Trail. This is a short but excellent segment of Trail. You can follow it for about one fourth mile where it will meet Highway 88. Notice the swales and numerous rust stained rocks. Modern vehicles have also used this segment. Return to your vehicle.

Our next stop will be Red Lake.

Between the Blue Lakes Road turn off and the Red Lake Road, the Trail is very difficult to follow due to erosion, highway construction and private land use.

Trail locations will be provided as available.

From the Blue Lakes Road proceed west.

At the Highway reset your odometer at the stop sign and proceed west.

NOTES

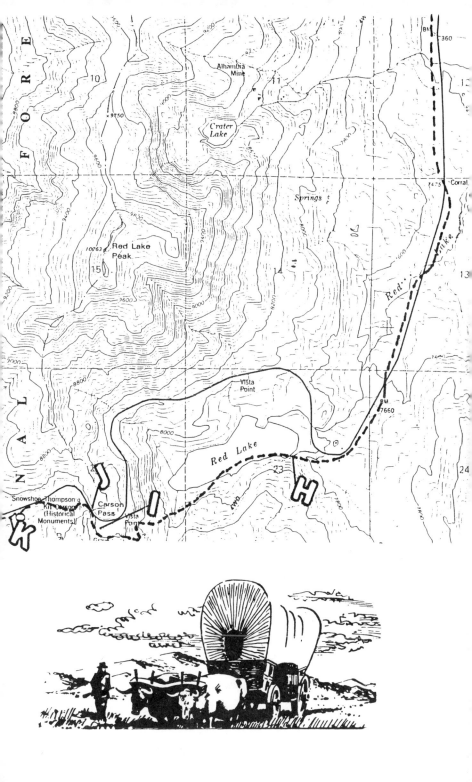

Devil's Ladder and Carson Pass Section

The mileages given in this section will be continuous from the Blue Lakes Road to Red Lake.

(OR represents odometer reading.)

OR .3 Trail crosses from the left to the right side of the Highway after leaving the meadow. There are some subtle traces in this area, but very hard to find.

OR 2.4 Wooden corral on your left.
Just past the corral the Trail crosses to the left side of the Highway.

OR 3.0 Strip sign on tree next to the right of Highway
<u>There is a convenient pullout lane on your right so you may slow down or stop.</u>
Here is the approximate location where the Trail crosses to the right of Highway. By looking back and across the highway you can see another strip sign on a dead tree. It indicates the Trail route. **From here to Red Lake the Trail is on posted private land.** The Trail will stay on the right side for about one half of a mile where it crosses to the left side of the Highway.

(H) OR 4.1 Red Lake Road Turn left
<u>Drive the short distance to the end of the paved road, turn around and park.</u>
This walking segment is 310 yards one-way.
Start down the dirt road to your right for 80 yards away from the lake. Turn left and walk 30 yards to the brown iron "T" marker. The gully is the Trail. Return to the lake and up on the earth filled dam for about 200 yards.

You now should get a good view across the lake and toward Carson Pass. The Trail traveled on the left side of the old lake. The first section of the Trail is under water now due to the dam on which you are standing. The Trail emerges from the lake three fourths of the way around the lake on the left side. We will tell you how to get to that point later.

The Trail works its way through the trees in the bowl above the far side of the lake.

... Tuesday, September 18. The summit of the great Sierra looms before us and must be passed today. Keeping up the mountain stream three miles brought us to a small lake nestled among high precipitous crags. The margin of the lake, called in some guide books "Red Lake," is fringed by a growth of rich grass. Passing around on the left or south side of the lake we begin the ascent of the first mountain or main dividing ridge. It was steep and rocky, so much so as to make me doubt whether the pioneer wagons can ever be dragged over it. ...

Bernard Reid, 1849

Return to your vehicle, **RESET THE ODOMETER** at the Highway and proceed west.

1.9 **John G. Meyer viewpoint pullout to the left.** There are some interesting historic interpretive signs and good photograph locations along this segment of the Highway looking down at Red Lake.

Return to your vehicle, reset the odometer and proceed west.

.3 Turn left onto an unmarked paved road just past the last overlook. **Be careful. This turn is on a curve and vehicles come very fast from the other direction.**

If you miss this turn, proceed west 100 yards and turn left into the Carson Pass parking area. Drive through and proceed back east on the Highway. This will return you to the turnoff.

(I) **.2** Drive to the end of the pavement and park in the large parking area. This is a beautiful walking segment but a very strenuous three fourths mile one-way. Just take your time, especially on the return walk up the mountain.

Remember to take your day pack, water and camera.

Aug. 8th. Thirsday, ... road tolerable good, passed a lake on our right Just before, reaching the foot of the mountains, the mountain is near 1 mile high and verry steep and rocky, we might Say almost perpendicular, it Beet anny thing that ever, I Saw, for waggons to pass over, however we came over, without takeing the second pull...

Leander Loomis 1850

You are now standing on one of the most spectacular pieces of Trail on the Carson River Route.

The "Devil's Ladder," as called by some, was mentioned in every emigrant diary. Actually, the emigrants had several names for this section of the Trail; Three-Quarter Mountain, First Summit, Dividing Ridge and others.

From the edge of the pavement, walk 35 yards down the old highway road bed.

The "new" Highway 88 was built in the 1960s.

Aug. 27th. 1850
... At the foot of this mountain was an iron safe that some
emigrant had started with, but when he got here and looked
up this mountain I expect he came to the conclusion that he
had haulded far enough, and I think it a wise conclusion.

Jerome Dutton.

Turn left and you will be looking down the very steep Trail. You may notice some tin markers on the trees indicating the Trail. You are standing on the road bed for the old highway and before that the Amador-Carson Valley Wagon Road.

Walk down the old roadway bank to the Trail and follow the Trail downhill about 100 yards. As the Trail curves to the right notice the rock alignment to the downhill edge where the Emigrants did a bit of Trail improvement. Continue down the Trail and enjoy a great view of Red Lake and the mountains.

You will come upon some slabs of granite that are the Trail. Note the rust stains on these rocks. You are now in the middle of the "Devils Ladder."

... we pushed up the step. The most astonishing thing

*respecting the road, is, that any man of common sense should
have first thought of taking a wagon over it. There is about a
half a mile of road that is nearly perpendicular as a horse
can well travel up alone, and the road is filled with large
blocks of granite as it is in the can[y]on below. Nearly half
way up is a sudden bend in the road and an increase, if
possible, of steepness. Below this mountain falls off almost in
a precipice. At the foot may be seen three wagons which
have run backwards and gone over, ...*

William Tell Parker, 1850

When you come to the trees, the Trail will make a wide sweeping switchback downhill. You will have to work through the trees. You should be able to see where others have gone. Follow the Trail down the side of the hill looking for rust stained rocks as you go. There are some very impressive samples in this area.

As you near the bottom, the Trail will start curving to the right. You will now be coming to a more open area. Staying to the right of a large rock outcropping, the Trail becomes very rocky for a few yards before it begins to curve left. The Trail then becomes gentle. This was a staging area for wagons before beginning the ascent of "Three-Quarter Mountain," as many emigrants referred to the climb to Carson Pass.

As you walk the Trail it will make a curve right and come to some willows at the edge of the creek. Work your way left, staying left of the creek and in just a few yards you will come to a more open area. Following the Trail you will come to a creek, cross it and stay right due to a very wet marshy area. After crossing the marshy area the Trail curves left and follows through a stand of trees just above the wet area. You will now descend a gentle hill toward the lake. The Trail obviously veers to the right and through the trees.

You may notice a metal Trail marker or two to your left. It seems that there were two trails through this area. Most likely the one near the creek was used in dry years and the one you are standing on for wet years. You should be able to see glimpses of Red Lake through the trees. The Trail is well beaten because those who fish, little to their knowledge, have been using the Emigrant Trail for a pathway to their favorite fishing spots.

After crossing a gully wash-out, continue for a short distance, but watch for the Trail veering left and into the lake. This is the location of the Trail referred to as being three fourths of the way through the lake when you were on the dam overlooking Red Lake.

You now can have the same experience of the emigrants by making the climb back up "The Devil's Ladder." Take your time and enjoy the walk. Remember, you are walking at an elevation of over 8,000 feet. If you complete this last hike down to Red Lake and back,
you are to be congratulated, for you will have

Conquered the Elephant.

When you return to the old highway roadbed, take the time to catch your breath before you continue walking the next segment of Trail.

The Trail continues 15 yards to your left and on the uphill side of the old highway. (It is about 50 yards east of the parking area pavement.) The Trail will climb the hill a short distance and curve to the right. Notice the two strip signs that indicate that it makes a turn to the right. Follow the Trail on a wonderful Class I segment for about 30 yards past the last turn. Here you will find a large pine tree just above the Trail with a metal Trail marker attached to it.

Rope Scar

This tree is in a direct line with the Trail leading down to Devil's Ladder. Many researchers believe that the notch on the uphill side of this tree, near its base, is the scar remaining from ropes and chains the emigrants used to assist moving the wagons up the steep slope. Some of the diaries spoke of such an effort.

Continue past the tree noticing the rock alignment on the downhill side of the Trail. This shows some Trail improvements that were made and you will notice they are similar to the rock alignments on Devil's Ladder. Look for possible rust stained rocks along the way.

About 50 yards past the rock alignment and set back into the trees a few yards is another iron "T" marker.

From the "T" marker, the Trail passes right of a large rock outcropping with names in white painted on it.

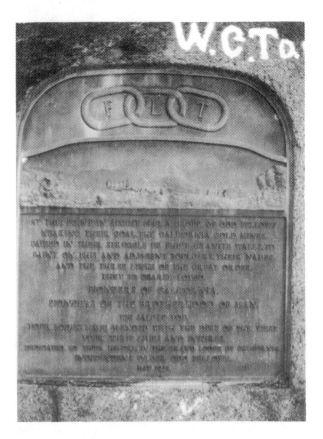

Also notice the beautiful brass plaque mounted on the rock face about 10 feet above the level of the Trail. An easy climb will take you to the plaque.

After you have finished exploring the area, continue along the Trail moving a bit to your right, where you come upon the Unknown Pioneer's grave.

From the grave turn right and follow the foot path to the paved road. Your vehicle will be down the hill to your right about 100 yards.

<u>Drive back to the Highway, reset the odometer, and turn west.</u>

(J)   .1   Carson Pass Visitors' Center parking area

<u>Turn left and drive .1 mile, approximately 100 yards, to the Carson Pass parking area and park.</u> If it is summertime, Memorial Day through Labor Day, the visitor station should be open. It is staffed by

volunteers from Eldorado National Forest Information Association. This is a good place to spend some time looking at maps, books and artifacts of the area.

At the far end of the parking lot is a tall granite monument in honor of Snowshoe Thompson.

To the left of the restrooms is a brass plaque, a replica of the Carson Tree blaze mounted on a slab of granite. There are a couple of errors on this marker.

The marker states, "Behind this marker stood the tree . . ." We know that this marker has been moved two, maybe three times for highway realignment and the tree was removed when it was widened.

It also states ". . . that the then guide of John C. Fremont . . ." Well, you may remember that on the expedition of 1843-1844, Kit Carson was hired as an Indian fighter and hunter. It was Thomas "Broken Hand" Fitzpatrick who was officially hired as the guide.

And last of all, I don't think that Carson carved his name on the tree in the winter of 1844. With the party starving and in a desperate situation, would one take the time to dig down through 20 to 30 feet of snow to ground level to carve his or her name?

If, in fact, Carson did carve his name on that tree, I believe it would have been in the summer of 1853 when he did return to Carson Pass. Carson was helping to herd some 6,500 sheep, that he bought for $1.50 per head in New Mexico. He brought them into California by way of the Carson River Route and hoped to sell them for $5.50 per head. This may have been when he carved his name on that tree.

You draw your own conclusions.

This walk is about one eighth mile one-way. To locate the Trail, walk to the right and back of the restrooms. It drops straight off the hill, behind the restroom and a bit to the right. Follow the metal trail markers on the trees. Because of the parking lot construction, the Trail is difficult to follow for the first few yards. But you should have good Trail finding skills by now and there are some good examples of rust stained rocks in this downhill section. As the Trail reaches the bottom, it veers right and is eventually lost under the Highway fill.

Return to your vehicle, reset the odometer and proceed west.

All distances will be continuous from Carson Pass as you exit the parking lot from the east end. DO NOT RESET THE ODOMETER UNTIL INSTRUCTED TO DO SO.

(OR represents Odometer Reading)

Approximately .1 mile after you pull out of the parking lot on the right is a wonderful rock wall built to support the old highway.

OR .2 Left turn onto old highway. At the west side of the meadow, you will turn left onto the old highway. This segment of road is falling into disrepair. However in 1997 I was able to drive my sedan down this road. You can always turn around if you find the going too rough.

OR .3 After your turn onto the old highway, the Trail will cross from left to right at .3 miles. This is not a well-defined piece of Trail so there is no need to spend much time here.

OR .4 The road will make a wide curve to the right and left. Just before it turns back to the left the Trail will cross from your right to your left. The Trail will now be the same as the road you are driving.

(K) OR .5 There is good parking on the left before the segment. Here is a short walking segment that veers left and down below the road. The walk is 150 yards one-way.

As you walk on this segment notice the rock wall supporting the old highway. The Trail will be at the edge of a meadow and gently curves back to the road.

Return to your vehicle and continue. The Trail is the same as the old road.

(L) OR .7 Parking on the edge of the road is a little tight, but is possible. Here is another excellent walking segment for about 200 yards one-way that veers left of the road.

Return to your vehicle the way you came and continue driving.

(M)   OR   1.0   The intersection of another dirt road appears on the right. Park on the far side of the intersection. Seek out a young pine tree with a metal diamond trail marker. Walk past this tree, across a drainage and look for a tree with a strip sign just right of the Trail. The walk is one third mile one-way.
From this marker, the Trail will swing left. Follow the Trail to its end where it meets the Highway.

Return to your vehicle and backtrack to the Highway by way you came.

When you stop at Highway 88, **RESET THE ODOMETER** and proceed west.

All distances will be continuous from this stop as you exit. DO NOT RESET THE ODOMETER UNTIL INSTRUCTED TO DO SO.   (OR represents Odometer Reading)

(N)   OR   1.1   Look for a strip sign on a tree to the right of the Highway and near the edge of the pavement. On the right, just past the strip sign is a short pullout area to park. You will be walking eastward on pristine Trail near the Highway for about one eighth mile one-way. Walk back to that strip sign, follow the direction of the strip sign and you should be able to discover the Trail.

... Monday 2nd We were off quite early this morning; expect today to have a view of the elephant ...

Andrew Hall Gilmore, 1850

When you reach the end of this segment, the Trail appears to fork. Stay right and look for a very impressive rust stained rock very near the edge of the Highway. The side of the rock facing the Highway has the best smoothing and polish. By aligning yourself with the Trail and looking across the Highway, you are facing the direction of the segment of Trail you followed from the previous stop.

Retrace your steps to the Highway and the strip sign. Stand left of the tree with the strip sign, look across the Highway, and observe the metal diamond Trail marker on a tree next to the Highway.

If you wish to follow the Trail, **carefully** cross Highway 88. It will follow for another one third mile one-way.
By following the Trail alignment and markers, you should be able to follow the Trail to its end in a wide gravel area near the highway.

Carefully retrace your steps to your vehicle and proceed west.

REMEMBER - DO NOT RESET THE ODOMETER

(O)   OR   1.8   <u>Turn sharply to your right on an old highway</u> <u>segment and park.</u> The Trail is the same as the old highway. By standing on the old highway, walk west over a slight rise in an open area. The walk is three fourths mile one-way.

You should be walking parallel to the Highway. And the Trail is not clear in this open area. As you cross the drainage, you should be able to see large juniper trees growing above the drainage. Walk up to the juniper trees and veer slightly left as you descend a gentle slope. You will enter an aspen grove. The Trail is well marked with metal markers for the next one half mile. Some searching may be necessary as this is a well vegetated area. The best time of year to see this section is after the snow melts in the spring or late in the fall after the leaves have dropped.

Near the end of this segment the Trail slopes towards the Highway. The Trail stays above a large boulder next to the pavement. It continues high above and parallel to the Highway for another 75 yards before heading down to cross to the left of Highway. There are some great rust stained and polished rocks in this open area.

The view over Caples Lake is spectacular from here. Little evidence of the Trail has been found below the Highway pavement to the lake.

47

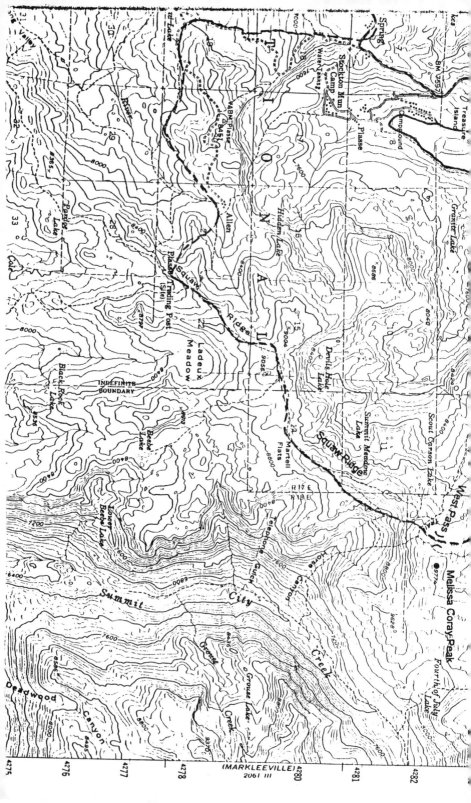

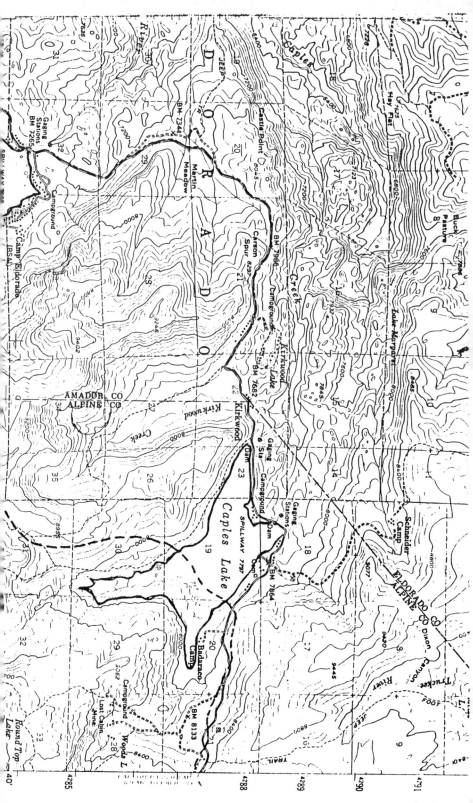

Return to your vehicle and proceed less than one mile to Schneider Cow Camp Road. This is also the CALTRANS Caples Lake Maintenance Station road.

Make a "U" turn here, stopping at the stop sign, **RESET THE ODOMETER** and proceed east

.1 Park at the historical marker on the right
By looking at the Trail map on the previous page you can see where the Trail leaves the Highway and heads in a southwesterly direction. The map shows the Trail's direction as it leaves the Caples Lake valley. Pacific Gas and Electric Company built dams in 1922 that flooded this valley. Most of the emigrants spent the night in this valley before climbing to West Pass, the highest point wagons ever reached (9,600 feet) in the westward migration.

Emigrant journals listed several different names for this area. Some called it Summit Lake. Others called it Mountain Lake, Lake Valley, or Meadow Lake. One journal mistakenly referred to it as Red Lake.

No matter what they called it, they all knew they were just days from the gold fields.

In 1849 California was not yet a state and therefore boundaries were up to one's own imagination. Most emigrants thought that when West Pass was crossed they would be in California. But there was much debate over the boundaries which weren't established until statehood on September 9, 1850.

The Caples family emigrated to California in 1849 over this very route and were so taken with this beautiful place that they returned and set up a homestead using it as a summer retreat for thirty years. They also sold goods to passing emigrants and gold seekers for many years. Caples Lake was named for them.

One of the Caples children died in 1864 and was buried in the old meadow. When the meadow was to be flooded, the grave was moved to higher ground. The grave is located in the summer home tract just west of the historical highway marker.

Looking at the photograph on page 50 West Pass and Melissa Coray Peak are seen on the ridge. The map on page 48/49 shows how the Trail continues over the ridge on the opposite side of Caples Lake into Emigrant Valley. The Trail moves up the shoulder of the ridge in a southerly direction until it reaches West Pass.

*... October 1st, 1849 - - The Summit is crossed! Far away in
the haze the dim outline of the Sacramento Valley are
discernible! We are on the down grade now and our
famished animals may pull us through. We are in the midst of
huge pines, so large as to challenge belief. .....*

Niles Searls

The Trail follows Squaw Ridge around the Silver Lake basin where it
rejoins the Highway at Tragedy Springs. Squaw Ridge was
abandoned as a wagon route in 1863.
After silver was discovered in Nevada in 1859 money was made
available by the California Legislature to build the Amador-Carson
Valley Wagon Road. In 1862 the Carson Spur was blasted through
and a more direct route by way of the Silver Basin was completed.

Return to your vehicle and reset the odometer.
In order to travel west safely, drive east **.4 mile** and turn right onto
the road for the Woods Creek parking area.
then make a "U" turn coming to a stop at the stop sign. Reset the
odometer and proceed west.

8.0   AGAIN reset the odometer when passing in front of Kay's
Resort just after the Silver Lake bridge-spillway.

*... August 2nd, Across the summit we stopped and let our
cattle rest whilst we took a hearty smoke of cigars which we
brought with us from the States ... We have been two days
crossing the Sierra Nevada range. The pass across the Sierra
Nevada is about 2,500 feet higher than the pass in the Rocky
Mountains ...*

Thomas Christy, 1850

NOTES

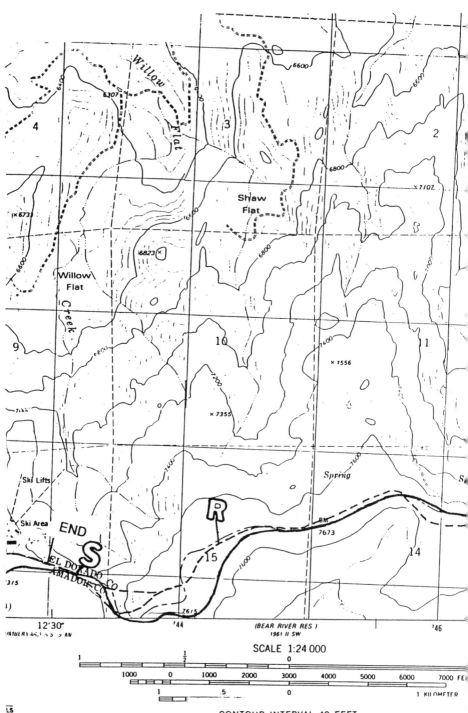

SCALE 1:24 000

CONTOUR INTERVAL 40 FEET
NATIONAL GEODETIC VERTICAL DATUM OF 1929

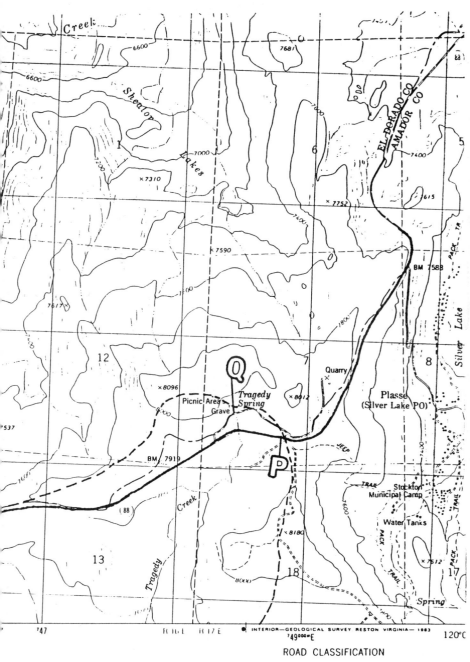

ROAD CLASSIFICATION

Primary highway,
hard surface

Secondary highway

Light-duty road, hard or
improved surface

2.3 **Carefully** pull left onto an unmarked overlook to park at the historical plaque. There is a historical plaque imbedded in a boulder overlooking Silver Lake. From here we can see West Pass, Melissa Coray Peak, and a short section of Squaw Ridge.

Who was Melissa Coray?

When forty-five men and one woman assembled in Pleasant Valley to begin their trek over the Sierra Nevada in the spring of 1848 that one woman was twenty-year-old Melissa Coray.

When Brigham Young requested volunteers to enlist in the Mormon Battalion, 23 year-old William Coray volunteered. Four days earlier, William had married eighteen-year-old Melissa Burton. She was not about to be left behind while her love, William, marched off to war. So Melissa enlisted in the Battalion as one of twenty washer - women. Together, William and Melissa began their six-month honeymoon walk to California.

When Battalion members were discharged in San Diego, July 1847 William and Melissa were in the group of 51 that traveled along the coast of California headed for Yerba Buena.

On October 2, 1847, after reaching Monterey, Melissa gave birth to a baby boy. He was named William, Jr. While on the march to San Diego, Melissa had been pregnant for one month having arrived in the latter part of January 1847.

The Corays were planning to continue to Yerba Buena when their hearts were broken when the baby became ill and died. The baby was buried in the Monterey cemetery. At the same time, William developed a cough that would never leave him.

The Corays stayed in Yerba Buena and earned money until June of 1848 when they found themselves in Pleasant Valley.

Nearly two years after enlisting in the Battalion, this young couple began to prepare for another long hard march, this time to the Salt Lake Valley and the end of their journey.

Melissa would be the only woman in this group of 45 men who would soon start on an adventure that history would remember as the first wagon train over the Sierra Nevada using the Carson River Route. She would be there when the historic names were given to Sly Park, Camp Creek and Leek Spring. She would be at Tragedy Spring to see the shocking discovery of the three dead scouts. She may have helped in the reburial and the naming of this site.

Melissa was the first recorded white woman to cross West Pass, Carson Pass and to enter Hope Valley. She was there when the Mormon party met the Clyman, Cornwall, Lassen and Chiles wagon parties heading for California.

She and William reached the settlement in the Salt Lake valley on October 6, 1848, two years, two months and sixteen days after they left for the march to California as members of the Mormon Battalion. The Corays soon purchased a plot of land. They began to build their house with much needed help from others due in part to William's poor health. They moved into their new home on January 20, 1849.

Melissa gave birth to a baby girl on February 6,1849. The Corays named her Melissa. Again, she had been pregnant during the difficult walk along the Trail.

She celebrated her twenty-first birthday March 2, 1849, and five days later, Melissa's sweetheart's health worsened and William died.

In three years, this young woman had enough experiences to last a lifetime. Driven from her home in Nauvoo, she walked across Iowa, and joined the Mormon Battalion just days after her marriage to stay with her husband. Melissa walked the 2,000 miles to San Diego, California, gave birth to a baby who soon died. Then she walked another 1,000 miles from San Diego to the Salt Lake Valley, Utah, and gave birth to another child, only to have her husband die.

December 25, 1851, Melissa remarried, becoming the second of four wives of William Kimball. Her marriage to Kimball would be for "Time" only, while her marriage to Coray was for "Eternity," according to Mormon Church doctrine.

In 1860 Kimball, Melissa and their 5 children moved to Parley's Park, 25 miles east of Salt Lake City. Here, they established a hotel and stage stop on the Overland Stage Route, now Interstate 80.

Melissa cooked gourmet meals for famous people, like Mark Twain, Horace Greely, and Walter Whitman, who stayed at this soon-to-become famous stage stop. Their eleven room native-stone building still stands today.

Melissa gave birth to her ninth and last child in 1866

Gold was discovered in the area in 1869 and a boomtown sprang up nearby, known today as Park City.

Melissa returned to Salt Lake City during the 1880's.

Sometime in the 1890's Melissa made a trip to California to visit some of the many places she and William had encountered in 1847. As she visited the Monterey cemetery, she became greatly discouraged when she could not locate the grave of her son, William, Jr.

Melissa passed away on September 21, 1903, at the age of 75 and was buried next to her "sweetheart," William Coray.

Melissa did not realize the large part she played in so many historic events even though she was honored numerous times for her contributions to history.

On July 30, 1994, two organizations, the Sons of the Utah Pioneers and the Oregon-California Trails Association, jointly dedicated the mountain peak that looks westward over West Pass to honor the memory of this most courageous pioneer woman.

Reset the odometer and proceed west.

(P)   .4   Turn right onto the old highway and park. To see the historical marker **walk carefully** across to the left side of Highway 88. This intersection brings you to a historical marker. This is the companion marker to the one at Caples Lake, #661, which lists West Pass at 9,460 feet, while this one, #662, lists the West Pass elevation at 9,640 feet. This clearly makes the point that historical roadside markers are often incorrect. Actually the modern-day measurements document the elevation closer to 9,550 feet. It all depends where one stands when taking the measurement.

Return to your vehicle, reset the odometer and continue west on the old highway.

.1   Grave site
In the meadow to the left of the pavement, you will see four round metal posts. This is the grave of an emigrant girl whose story will be told at the Maiden's Grave's stop. Continue west on the old highway.

(Q)   .2   Reset the odometer and continue west on the old highway and park at Tragedy Spring near the rock wall. The walk is one and one half miles one-way if you choose to walk the entire segment from here.

The story of Tragedy Spring is told in the Brief History section, starting on page 6, in the front of the guide book.

To locate the grave and the Spring, follow the foot path just left of the rock wall.

... Thursday July 20th. Yesterday we travailed about eight miles when we came to the place where the Brethren were supposed to have been killed and thrown into that hole, and covered with dirt by the Indians. After examining till we were sure that they were all three there, we again covered them up, ... In the morning fifteen of the men went after the horses, and those that stayed built a wall around the place where the Brethren were buried, and filled it up level with stone inside. And on a tree close by was engraven by Hudson....

Azariah Smith, 1848 (With the first Mormon party)

The Trail can be found 25 yards past the spring house. As you pass between two large trees, the Trail is to the left. Look for a diamond Trail marker on a tree and follow the foot path for about 150 yards out of the trees and through the open rock field. Watch for diamond Trail markers on small fir trees.

The deep foot path is actually a horse trail that will lead to the right at the top of the ridge. The Trail swings left into an open flat area. There are some very impressive grooved, rust stained, and polished rocks here. The diamond Trail markers will continue to guide you as the Trail proceeds directly west to the other side of the open area past a large fallen tree. Follow the Trail through a fence line as it curves left going gently downhill revealing a beautiful swale. This is a well marked beautiful hiking segment for about one and one half miles which leads to the other Maiden's Grave.

How many rocks with both grooves and rust stains along this

segment can you discover?

When you have finished exploring this segment of the Trail, retrace your steps to your vehicle.

Proceed west on the old highway until it rejoins the Highway. Reset the odometer at the stop sign and proceed west.

All distances will be continuous from the stop sign. DO NOT RESET THE ODOMETER UNTIL INSTRUCTED TO DO SO.
(OR represents Odometer Reading)

OR   1.2   Maiden's Grave and Devil's Garden Overlook.
Pull to the far right to park. Here you can enjoy the view and observe the grave markers.

The Maiden's Grave(s) Stories

In 1904 or 1905 a camper met an elderly woman and a younger woman in the Tragedy Spring's meadow. The elderly woman was searching for the grave of her young daughter whom she buried in

1850. During their conversation with the camper, the woman shared her story of being part of an emigrant wagon train heading for California when her daughter became ill and died. This woman was certain this was the meadow and that the grave was at the base of a large fir tree.

All three of them searched the meadow, but no grave could be found. The woman left saddened for her intent was to remove her daughter's remains and give her a proper Christian burial elsewhere.

The camper most likely spread the story of his encounter with this broken-hearted woman. Consequently, some people staying at the Kirkwood Inn took up a collection to pay for a carved headstone to read:

RACHEL MELTON

DIED OCT. 4, 1850

NATIVE OF IOWA

ERECTED BY GUESTS

AT KIRKWOOD

1908

At this point in time, the only visible grave in the area was one about 2 miles west of Tragedy Spring. The headstone was placed at this location.

It was about 1913 that a California State road worker, named Stephen Ferrari, was clearing and burning brush in the meadow by Tragedy Spring. The burned area exposed an outline of a grave marked by stones with a rock pile at the head.

Could this have been the grave the grief-stricken woman searched for some eight years prior? The grave site now marked with the metal posts?

And, what about the other grave?   Who is buried there?

In 1990 under a contract with the United States Forest Service, Chief Historian Kenneth Owens, Professor at Sacramento State University, discovered an entry in the Annals of Iowa *"Crossing the Plains in 1850,"* by William Edmundson. It reads as follows:

"OCTOBER 4,---- After traveling 6 miles, we came to a place called Tragedy Spring from three men having been killed there by the Indians; from the inscription on a tree close by,

they were killed on the night of the 27 Th of June, 1848.
There names were Daniel Browett, Ezra H. Allen and
Henderson Cox. They were all buried in one grave under a
pile of stones. After traveling two miles farther we came to a
trading post about noon where we camped having come eight
miles today. A young man from Henry County, named Allen
Melton, died at this place during the night."

According to local residents, as late as 1880, a wooden headboard
marked the grave of Allen Melton. So now we have the name
"Melton."

What about the name "Rachel?"

Could the elderly woman have mentioned the name of Rachel to the
camper at the Tragedy Spring's meadow that summer of 1905?

It seems conclusive that the facts reveal that it is Allen Melton who
is buried along the Highway 88 in what is signed "Maiden's Grave."
Perhaps someone someday will discover the name of the young
maiden buried in the grave at Tragedy Spring meadow.

The Trail crosses to the left side of the Highway past the Maiden's
Grave marker.

**Proceed west and remember DO NOT RESET THE
ODOMETER.**

OR   1.7   The Trail crosses to the right side of the Highway and
will stay on the right side until the Mormon Carson Trail road turn
off .

OR   2.4   Turn right onto an unmarked paved service road.
Immediately turn left onto the Trail and the old highway roadbed.
The Trail drifts left, but the evidence is poor in this section.

OR   2.9   Follow the roadbed to a fork at 2.9 miles. Stay to the
left.

R) OR 3.0 The Trail will cross the dirt road from left to right going uphill. A strip sign can be seen on a tree on the uphill side of the road. <u>Drive to the top of the hill and park.</u> The walk is 3/4 mile one-way if you walk the entire segment from here.

Walk to the tree with the strip sign and follow the trail uphill, over the top of the ridge and down a very steep slope. There is a very impressive swale in this area but a bit difficult to find. There are few metal Trail markers in this area, but again, they are difficult to find.

When you are finished exploring this area, return to your vehicle.

do not recommend following the old highway from this point unless you have a 4 WD.

Return to the Highway the way you came. **NOW RESET THE ODOMETER** as you enter the Highway and proceed west.

S) 1.1 <u>Pull off to the right of the Highway and park.</u>
You should see some Trail markers on a tree just above the pavement. By parking on the shoulder, you can follow the Trail uphill into the trees. There are a few metal trail markers but they are difficult to locate and only traces of the Trail remain.

Reset odometer and proceed west.

2 Mormon Emigrant Trail Road <u>Turn off to the right.</u>
In less than 100 yards after the turnoff you should see a brown iron "T" marker to the right next to the pavement. From here the Trail follows this road (somewhat) all the way to Pleasant Valley and on into Placerville. Placerville was the town referred to as Hangtown in Mary Jane Caples' written remembrance of the end of the Trail in 1849.

...A few days later we arrived at the hill looking down on Hangtown; the end of our journey - and the Mecca of the emigrant - just 5 months and 6 days from the time of starting; tired, hungry, and travel stained but full of hope that we

could accumulate a few thousand and return to the dear old home and loved ones - for not one in 10,000 thought of remaining in California to make a home...

This completes the goal of this guide
which was to help you discover this section of the

Gold Rush Trail.

If you are like so many others,
your interest in locating emigrant wagon trails

may be just beginning . . .

SUGGESTED READING for the CARSON RIVER ROUTE

Archaeological and Historical Investigation of the Mormon-Carson Emigrant Trail, Eldorado and Toiyabe National Forests, Volume II: History Appendix A: - Compiled and Edited by Kenneth N. Owens. Professional Archaeological Services, Paradise, California; prepared under USNF Eldorado National Forest, Placerville, California, 1989

Bigler's Chronicle of the West - Erwin G. Gudde. University of California Press, Berkeley and Los Angeles, California, 1962

*Melissa's Journey with the Mormon Battalion - Norma Baldwin Ricketts. Utah Printing Company, Salt Lake City, Utah, 1994

Snowshoe Thompson - The Carson Valley Historical Society, Minden, Nevada, 1991

*The California Trail - Yesterday and Today - William E. Hill. Pruett Publishing Company, Boulder, Colorado, 1986

*The Gold Discovery Journal of Azariah Smith - Azariah Smith, ed. David L. Bigler. University of Utah Press, Salt Lake City, 1990

*The Mormon Battalion U.S. Army of the West, 1846-1848 - Norma Baldwin Ricketts. Utah State University Press, Logan, 1996

*The Road From El Dorado: The 1848 Trail Journal of Ephraim Green - ed. William Bagley. The Prairie Dog Press, Salt Lake City, Utah, 1991

*To the Land of Gold and Wickedness - Lorena Hayes, ed. Jeanne Hamilton Watson. The Patrice Press, St. Louis, Missouri, 1988

*Tragedy Spring and the Pouch of Gold - Norma Baldwin Ricketts. Rickets Publishing Company, Sacramento California, 1983

GENERAL READING

Brigham Young: American Moses - Leonard J. Arrington. University of Illinois Press, Urbana and Chicago, 1986

Fool's Gold, Captain John Sutter: Sacramento Valley's Sainted Sinner - Richard Dillon. Coward-McCann Inc., New York, 1967

*Ghost Trails to California - Tom Hunt. Nevada Publications, Las Vegas, Nevada, 1980

History of the Donner Party: A Tragedy of the Sierra - C. F. McGlashan. Stanford University Press, Stanford, California, 1947

Men to Match My Mountains - Irving Stone. Doubleday & Company, New York, 1956; The Berkley Publishing Group, New York, 1982

Ordeal by Hunger - George R. Stewart. Houghton Mifflin Company, Boston, Massachusetts, 1960; Pocket Books, New York, 1974

Sam Brannan: Builder of San Francisco - Louis J. Stellman. Exposition Press, New York, 1953

The California Gold Rush: Overland Diary of Byron N. McKinstry 1850-1852 - Bruce L. McKinstry. The Arthur H. Clark Company, Glendale, California, 1975

The California Trail: An Epic with Many Heroes - George R. Stewart. University of Nebraska Press, Lincoln and London, 1983

The Mormon Battalion in the Mexican War - Sgt. Daniel Tyler. The Rio Grande Press Inc., Chicago, Illinois, 1964

*The Wake of the Prairie Schooner - Irene D. Paden. The Macmillian Company, New York, 1943

The World Rushed In. The California Gold Rush Experience. An Eye Witness Account of a Nation Heading West - Wm. Swain. ed. J. S. Holiday. Simon and Schuster, New York, 1981

The Year of Decision 1846 - Bernard DeVoto. Houghton Mifflin Company, Boston, 1943

*They Saw the Elephant. Women in the California Gold Rush - JoAnn Levy. Shoe String Press, Hamden, Connecticut, 1990

*Trail of the First Wagons Over the Sierra Nevada (A Guide) - Charles K. Graydon. The Patrice Press, Gerald, Missouri, 1986

*Winter of Entrapment: A New Look at the Donner Party - Joseph A. King. P.D. Meany Publishers, Toronto, Ontario, Canada, 1993

* Indicates a member of the Oregon-California Trails Association (OCTA)

OCTA is an organization dedicated to the research and the preservation of emigrant trails, to educate the public about the wonders of the Trail and the necessity of preserving them, including supporting local, state and national legislation. Oregon-California Trails Association*524 South Osage Street*Post Office Box 1019*Independence MO 64051-0519*Phone (816) 252-2276*Fax (816) 836-0989*E-Mail octahqts@gvi.net rank has been a volunteer historian working with the Eldorado National Forest, mador Ranger District, on the Carson Pass segment of the California Trail since)78. Frank is a para-professional archaeologist recognized by the United States orest Service. Frank led the USFS and Sonoma State University on an ·chaeology survey of the Carson River Route segment of the California Trail.

rank continues his work under Volunteer Agreements with the Toiyabe National orest and the Eldorado National Forest mapping and doing field research. He is 1 "on call" Trail volunteer consultant for Cal-Trans, utility companies, the ski ·sorts all wishing to honor the Trail or keep peace with members of the Oregon-alifornia Trail Association or OCTA. He was awarded OCTA's prestigious)utstanding Educator for the Post Secondary Level for 1997."

rank, a native of Jackson, California, is a retired educator from the Amador ounty Unified School District. Besides giving tours, slide show presentations and ading hikes for 20 plus years, he has had a life time appreciation of and a ·owing knowledge of the Sierra Nevada flora and fauna.

rank personally escorted author David Nevin to local areas used by John C. ·remont in February of 1844. His help is acknowledged in Nevin's best seller book ·REAM WEST, later to become a TV mini-series.

rank is an instructor for Elderhostel employed by both the Sacramento Jazz ociety in Sacramento and University of the Pacific, at the Feather River Inn, lairsden, CA. His wife, Mary Ann, joins him during the living history portions of is class.

rank is a Charter and a Life Member of the 15-year-old OCTA. He was the first ·resident of the CA-NV Chapter of OCTA. He served as a tour guide on the ·arson Pass Tour for OCTA's 1986 convention in Carson City, NV., also as the ·our Director for the Gold Country Tour for the 1991 convention in Sacramento, ·A., and presently on the planning committee for the 1999 convention, Chico, CA.

·ank's slide presentation of the Emigrant Trail from Independence, Missouri, to langtown (Placerville), California, uses modern slides taken personally by Frank lus copies of some prints and paintings of old. Mary Ann reads excerpts from ·riginal diaries during the program.

Wagon Wheel Tours has become Frank's retirement venture. For information ·n his tour guide areas of specialization and his tour, speaking, or program ·cheduling contact him at Wagon Wheel Tours*12544 Eldel Road*Pine Grove ·A 95665-9718*Phone & Fax (209) 296-7242*E-Mail wagnwhel@volcano.net

NOTES

NOTES